A MINNESOTA Christmas

by Ryan Jacobson
illustrations by Shachi Kale

Adventure Publications, Inc.
Cambridge, MN

DEDICATIONS

For my grandparents, Jay and Joyce, and Cliff and Melba, who always made Christmas so very memorable and special.

—Ryan Jacobson

I would like to dedicate this book to my two boys, Shantanu and Ishaan, who have helped in the making of this book with their insightful suggestions, their enthusiasm, and for being such wonderful models! As with most things in my life, I couldn't have done this without the support and encouragement of my husband, Vikram.

—Shachi Kale

Cover and book design by Jonathan Norberg

10 9 8 7 6 5 4 3 2 1

Copyright 2013 by Ryan Jacobson and Shachi Kale
Published by Adventure Publications, Inc.
820 Cleveland Street South
Cambridge, MN 55008
1-800-678-7006
www.adventurepublications.net
All rights reserved
Printed in China

ISBN: 978-1-59193-446-2

A MINNESOTA Christmas

A Minnesota Christmas is like no other. The warmth of the season arrives to offset the cold. Winter's isolation is trumped by family and friends, who come together to celebrate Christmas traditions . . .

$\mathcal{W}$ith Thanksgiving over
and Black Friday spent, it's
finally time to decorate the house.
The chill in the air forewarns you
of the frigid temperatures to come.

❈ ❈ ❈

*The first snowfall brings
a magical day. Extra time
is enjoyed outdoors—but it's
still not enough. The kids beg,
"Just a little longer."*

❄ ❄ ❄

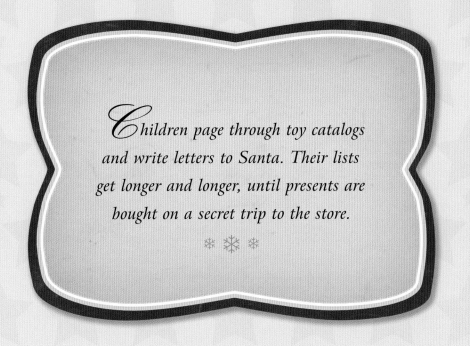

Children page through toy catalogs and write letters to Santa. Their lists get longer and longer, until presents are bought on a secret trip to the store.

❄ ❄ ❄

Opinions differ on whether the Christmas tree should be skinny or stout. A compromise is reached before frostbite settles in.

❄ ❄ ❄

Everyone enjoys the sweet side of Christmas. Little ones help to make Krumkake, baked cookies and homemade ice cream.

❄ ❄ ❄

On nighttime drives or while candlelight skiing, you marvel at all the beautiful lights. An evening stroll around a frozen lake makes for a better show than even the Holidazzle parade.

❄ ❄ ❄

Old friends make extra efforts to stay in touch. Even a greeting card from Florida can't make you wish you weren't here.

❄ ❄ ❄

*Y*ou give thanks
that the Christmas Pageant
is indoors this time. The
costumes don't fit over that
bulky winter gear.

❄ ❄ ❄

Familiar melodies—shared with family, friends, acquaintances and even strangers—serve to warm the heart and clear the mind.

A road trip to Grandpa and Grandma's is postponed because of chicken pox or the flu. Instead, the entire vacation is spent in pajamas.

*Snow falling on Christmas
Eve is an extra blessing, as you
share in the light of songs sung
by candlelight. Some services
are even conducted in Swedish,
Norwegian or German.*

❄ ❄ ❄

Children lie awake, worrying that Santa won't make it through the blizzard. They sneak out of bed to see if he's arrived yet.

❄ ❄ ❄

While Mom makes lefse
and Dad shovels snow, children dig
under the tree in search of their gifts.
After breakfast and pictures, it will
finally be time to see what's inside.

❄ ❄ ❄

*The day isn't complete
without a traditional game of
snow football at the local park or
ice hockey at a nearby pond.*

❄ ❄ ❄

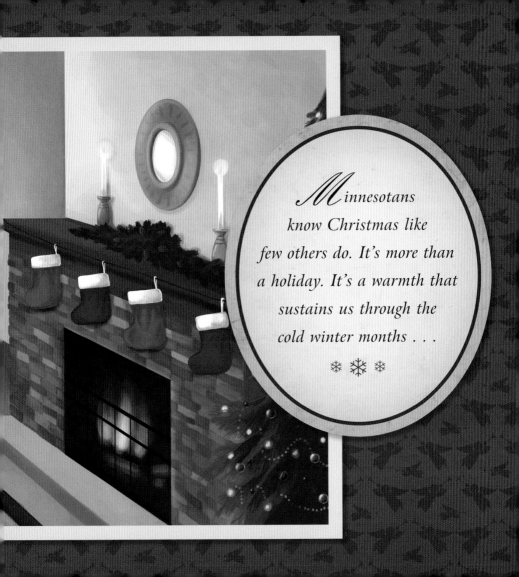

*M*innesotans
know Christmas like
few others do. It's more than
a holiday. It's a warmth that
sustains us through the
cold winter months . . .

❄ ❄ ❄

ABOUT THE AUTHOR

A lifelong Minnesotan, Ryan Jacobson has fond memories of Christmas. From celebrating Grandpa's birthday on Christmas Eve to eating homemade ice cream and playing football on an old gravel road, the traditions helped to make each year special. (The presents didn't hurt either!) Now all grown up, Ryan takes pride in writing books that inspire readers and capture their imaginations. He has written more than thirty books, including children's books, comic books and ghost stories. Ryan's also built a successful career as a presenter and has performed at well over a hundred schools, organizations and special events. He lives in Mora, Minnesota, with his wife and two sons. For more about the author, please visit www.RyanJacobsonOnline.com.

ABOUT THE ILLUSTRATOR

Shachi Kale grew up in Mumbai, the New York of India, a dynamic, alive and colorful city. She always had a passion for children's books and wanted to be a children's book illustrator all her life. She studied Applied Art at The Sophia Polytechnic and then started her career in the world of advertising. Soon after, Shachi started her own design studio and got the opportunity to illustrate, design and print her first three children's books. She moved to the United States in 2001 with her husband and has been a resident of Arizona since. Shachi has been lucky enough to illustrate more books, to work on several challenging design projects and to spend her days with her two boys. Books are an escape into other worlds, and Shachi happily escaped into the cold and snowy landscapes of Minnesota during a record hot summer in Arizona!